How to use your Snap Revi ok

This Writing Snap Workbook will help you to ɡ   AQA English Language exam. Questions and activities are divided into clear sections to work through and fully prepare for the exam.

Revise 1, 2 and 3
Short tasks progressing in level as you work through the topic.

Extend
More challenging activities to prepare you for the exam practice questions later in the book.

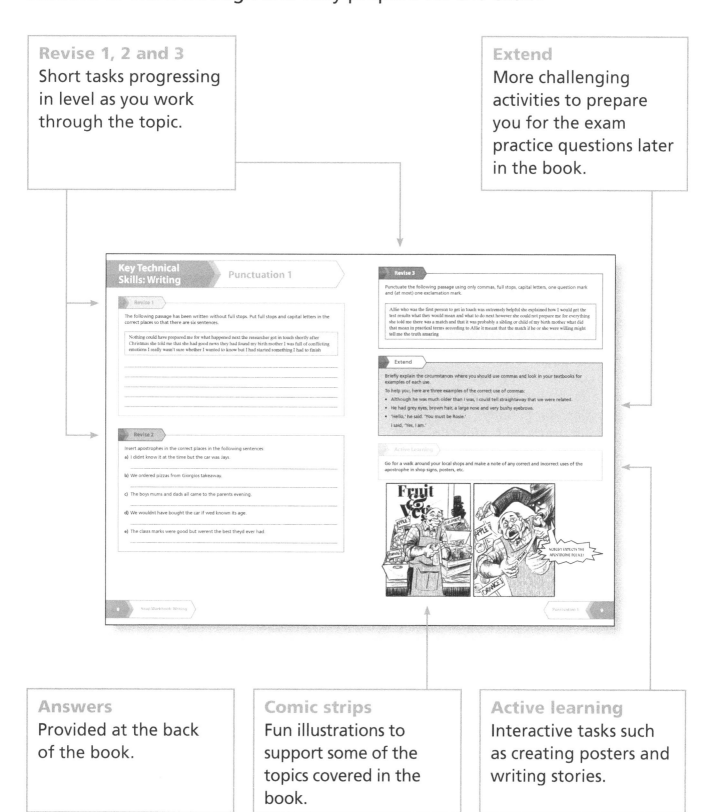

Answers
Provided at the back of the book.

Comic strips
Fun illustrations to support some of the topics covered in the book.

Active learning
Interactive tasks such as creating posters and writing stories.

AUTHOR: PAUL BURNS

Published by Collins
An imprint of HarperCollins*Publishers*
1 London Bridge Street
London SE1 9GF

© HarperCollins*Publishers* Limited 2019

ISBN 9780008355333

First published 2019

10 9 8 7 6 5 4 3 2 1

British Library Cataloguing in Publication Data.

A CIP record of this book is available from the British Library.

Commissioning Editor: Claire Souza
Managing Editor: Shelley Teasdale
Author: Paul Burns
Copyeditor and project management: Fiona Watson
Typesetting: Jouve India Private Limited
Cover designers: Kneath Associates and Sarah Duxbury
Inside concept design: Ian Wrigley
Illustrations: Rose and Thorn Creative Services Ltd
Production: Karen Nulty
Printed in the UK by Ashford Colour Press Ltd.

ACKNOWLEDGEMENTS
The author and publisher are grateful to the copyright holders for permission to use quoted materials and images.

Every effort has been made to trace copyright holders and obtain their permission for the use of copyright material. The author and publisher will gladly receive information enabling them to rectify any error or omission in subsequent editions. All facts are correct at time of going to press.

MIX
Paper from
responsible source
FSC www.fsc.org **FSC™ C007454**

This book is produced from independently certified FSC™ paper to ensure responsible forest management.

For more information visit:
www.harpercollins.co.uk/green

Contents

Revise 1

The following passage contains ten incorrect spellings. Find and highlight them, then write the correct spellings below.

> On Saturday I whent to the cinema with my freind. After we bort are tickets we saw a women who lives next door to me. She sed she had seen the movie and it was grate so she woz going to see it agen. She was rite. It was really good.

....

....

....

....

Revise 2

Insert the correctly spelled word into each of the following pairs of sentences:

a) **who's/whose**

Can you tell me .... hat that is on the floor?

It belongs to Joey, ... my cousin.

b) **are/our**

We .... going to Ishram's house after school today.

Tomorrow he's coming to .... house.

c) **its/it's**

I didn't buy it because .... not to my taste.

I didn't like .... price either.

d) **your/you're**

I think .... a better runner than I am.

Could I have .... autograph please?

e) **write/right**

I am going to .... a story about the moon.

I'm worried about getting my facts ....

f) **break/brake**

I tried to .... but I was too late and hit the lamppost.

Sometimes you need a .... from studying.

Put the following words into their plural forms:

a) key ....

b) piano ....

c) sheep ....

d) cactus ....

e) catch ....

f) wish ....

g) chimney ....

h) quantity ....

i) arena ....

j) glass ....

k) potato ....

l) soliloquy ....

Extend

The following paragraphs include spelling errors. Find the errors, highlight them and then re-write the paragraphs with the correct spellings.

I have decided to wright my autobiography. I have had a relatively short but, I think, definately interesting life. I never new who my mother and farther wear because I was abandoned on the steps of the locale hospital when I was only a few days old. Fortunitely I was found by a sirgeon who was doing a nite shift at the hospital and took me in. Otherwise, I dread to imagine what might have occured.

For quiet a long time my storey was in the paper almost every day. The nurses had cristened me 'Rosie' and their were frequent appeels for Rosie's parents to come forward but nobody ever did. Eventually I was fosterd and then adopted by my Mum and Dad. I love them but I have always been fascinated by my wierd background and so was very exited when I was approached by a television company who wanted to use my DNA to find out the truth.

Active Learning

Make a poster to remind yourself of how to spell any of the following words that you find difficult: separate, because, necessary, exaggerate.

Revise 1

Insert the correctly spelled word into each of the following sentences:

a) advise/advice

I .... you to do more revision.

Thank you. That's good ....

b) were/where/we're

Tell me .... you're going.

We .... going to go to town.

But .... staying in instead.

c) practise/practice

.... makes perfect.

I really need to .... my spellings.

d) there/their/they're

I support them because .... the best.

I'm never going .... again.

It was .... best performance ever.

e) flower/flour

You need 500 grams of .... for the recipe.

There was a single .... in a vase.

f) stationery/stationary

We need more ...., especially envelopes and paper.

The vehicle was .... when I approached it.

Revise 2

Put the following verbs into their simple past forms.

a) permit .... **b)** greet ....

c) travel .... **d)** reveal ....

e) regret .... **f)** visit ....

g) happen .... **h)** entertain ....

i) cancel .... **j)** recur ....

k) succeed ....

Read the following definitions and use your dictionary to help you work out what the word is, then complete and correctly spell the word.

a) ac __ __ __ __ __ __ __ __ __ __   (noun) lodgings

b) tr __ __ __ __ y   (noun) a play that is not a comedy

c) pr __ v __ __ __ ge   (noun) having an advantage over others

d) di __ __ __ __ __ __ a   (noun) a very unpleasant result of eating bad food

e) oc __ __ __ __ __ __ __ __ __ y   (adverb) every now and again

f) su __ __ __ __ __ __ __ l   (adjective) achieving the desired outcome

g) eup __ __ __ __ __ __ __ c   (adjective) using mild or pleasant words to refer to things which people may find unpleasant, upsetting or embarrassing to talk about

h) au __ __ __ __ __ __ __ __ __ __ e   (adjective) reliable/coming from someone with power or influence

In a few sentences, explain the rules or patterns that might help with these spelling problems. Give examples for each.

a) the spelling of 'ee' sounds: ie or ei

b) how to change single nouns ending in 'y' into their plural forms and verbs ending in 'y' to the third-person singular form ending in 's'

c) whether or not to double a consonant before adding 'ed' or 'ing'

d) when to add 'es' rather than 's' to form a plural

e) how to change nouns ending in 'o' into their plural forms.

Look back at written work you have done during the past year, particularly practice exam papers. Make a list of all the words that you spelled incorrectly and learn the correct spellings.

The following passage has been written without full stops. Put full stops and capital letters in the correct places so that there are six sentences.

> Nothing could have prepared me for what happened next the researcher got in touch shortly after Christmas she told me that she had good news they had found my birth mother I was full of conflicting emotions I really wasn't sure whether I wanted to know but I had started something I had to finish

Insert apostrophes in the correct places in the following sentences:

a) I didnt know it at the time but the car was Jays.

b) We ordered pizzas from Giorgios takeaway.

c) The boys mums and dads all came to the parents evening.

d) We wouldnt have bought the car if wed known its age.

e) The classs marks were good but werent the best theyd ever had.

Punctuate the following passage using only commas, full stops, capital letters, one question mark and (at most) one exclamation mark.

Allie who was the first person to get in touch was extremely helpful she explained how I would get the test results what they would mean and what to do next however she could not prepare me for everything she told me there was a match and that it was probably a sibling or child of my birth mother what did that mean in practical terms according to Allie it meant that the match if he or she were willing might tell me the truth amazing

Extend

Briefly explain the circumstances where you should use commas and look in your textbooks for examples of each use.

To help you, here are three examples of the correct use of commas:

- Although he was much older than I was, I could tell straightaway that we were related.
- He had grey eyes, brown hair, a large nose and very bushy eyebrows.
- 'Hello,' he said. 'You must be Rosie.'

  I said, 'Yes, I am.'

Active Learning

Go for a walk around your local shops and make a note of any correct and incorrect uses of the apostrophe in shop signs, posters, etc.

Revise 1

Draw lines to match the following punctuation marks with their definitions:

brackets	Used to show the omission of words from a sentence or to show a thought trailing off.
ellipsis	Used to indicate speech, titles or quotations.
dash	Put around additional bits of information in a sentence.
inverted commas	Used to show an interruption to the train of thought.

Revise 2

Each of the following sentences needs at least one comma, colon or semi-colon. Insert the correct punctuation mark where indicated by *.

a) The candle flickered * the coals spluttered.

b) The house grew dark * the power had failed.

c) Despite the dim light * we carried on talking.

d) There was plenty to talk about * our plans for the holiday * what we were going to eat * and what would happen if power wasn't restored.

e) Finally * Jim * who was the oldest of the group * decided to look under the stairs for the fuse box.

f) 'There's a torch here *' he said * 'so I should be able to see what the problem is.'

The following passage contains punctuation errors. Find the errors, highlight them and then re-write the passage with the correct punctuation.

> Its quite a big house, the owners rented it to us while they were away. Jim who knew them quite well had made all the arrangements. I didnt know anyone else there except Maria however they all seemed very pleasant. I'd had a bit of trouble finding it; it was quite dark when I got off the bus.

Extend

The following passage tells part of a story using indirect speech. Re-write it using direct speech, making sure that you set it out properly and use the correct punctuation.

> Suddenly, we heard a strange noise. Alesha asked Jim whether it was him. He asked her what she meant. She replied that someone had made a noise and it must have been him. Jim said that he hadn't made any sound but he had found the torch. Gary whispered that if it wasn't Jim it must have been a ghost because it certainly wasn't any of the group. Maria was quite angry and told us all that we were being silly and there's no such thing as ghosts. Then we heard it again.

Active Learning

Look back at some of your old essays and practice exam answers. Pick out any errors in punctuation and make sure that you know what the correct punctuation should have been.

Revise 1

Look at the following simple sentences and use different colours to highlight the following elements: subject, object, main verb, preposition, agent. Note that not all of the sentences contain all of the elements.

a) We ate the pies.

b) The massive dog barked at the moon.

c) All the plates were washed by Jim.

d) Nobody likes a know-all.

e) Maria found the torch in the bin.

Revise 2

Change the following sentences from the active to the passive voice:

a) We bought the pies at the corner shop.

_____

_____

b) They all enjoyed the holiday.

_____

_____

c) The dog ate the last pie.

_____

_____

Change these sentences from passive to active:

d) Before we left, the house was cleaned from top to bottom.

_____

_____

e) I was scared by the noises.

_____

_____

f) The fridge had been filled with delicious snacks.

_____

_____

Indicate whether each of the following sentences is a minor, simple, compound or complex sentence.

a) I put out the bins and Gary vacuumed the floors. ....

b) After he had finished in the kitchen, Jim went upstairs to pack. ....

c) Alesha and Maria wrote a note to the landlord. ....

d) Home at last. ....

Extend

Write a short account (two or three paragraphs) of a trip you have been on, making sure that you use at least one complex, one compound, one simple and one minor sentence. Use the passive voice at least once.

Active Learning

Choose a textbook or revision guide and look for examples of all the different kinds of sentences that have been mentioned above.

Revise 1

Combine the following sentences to form complex sentences using the conjunctions **because**, **despite**, **before** and **unless**. For one of the sentences you will need to change the form of one of the verbs.

a) I chose that book. It is by my favourite author.

_____

b) I had breakfast. I went to school.

_____

c) I will not lend it to you. You promise to give it back next week.

_____

d) I revised for hours last night. I still couldn't do the test.

_____

Revise 2

Combine the following sentences to form complex sentences using relative pronouns.

a) Mrs Arbuthnot lives next door. She promised to help me revise.

_____

_____

b) I stayed up working until one o'clock. It turned out to be a mistake.

_____

_____

c) I'm going to meet Jo. I have known her since primary school.

_____

_____

d) The apples were all sold. I grew them.

_____

_____

Re-write the following passage to make it more effective. Use a variety of simple, compound and complex sentences (adding or changing words if necessary).

> I walked to the nearest bus stop. I met Jo there. She told me that she couldn't go to town with me. Her cat was ill. She had to take him to the vet's. I don't really like animals. I offered to go with her. She said that was very kind. She preferred to go alone. I got the impression that she was not telling the truth. I left the bus stop. I felt a bit guilty. I had not trusted her. I decided to follow her.

Extend

Look at a piece of creative writing that you have done in the last year. Go through it and see if you can improve it by using a greater variety of sentence structures.

Active Learning

To make sure you're clear about their use, use the internet to find definitions of the following terms: conjunction, relative pronoun, active voice, passive voice, subordinate clause.

Revise 1

Indicate which of the following are reasons for starting a new paragraph:

a) A change of speaker when using direct speech. ☐

b) Getting to the end of the page. ☐

c) A change of topic or subject matter. ☐

d) Introducing a new character. ☐

e) A change of time or place. ☐

f) Feeling like a rest. ☐

Revise 2

Read the following sentences and underline the discourse markers.

a) As soon as I knew what had happened, I knew we had to act. ☐

b) Many people, however, do not agree with me. ☐

c) Furthermore, they have no appetite for action. ☐

d) Consequently, we have decided to go ahead without them. ☐

e) Finally, we came up with a plan. ☐

Now write the numbers 1 to 5 in the boxes beside each sentence to indicate whether the marker is used to:

1) express cause and effect

2) express passing time

3) give order or sum up

4) introduce a contrasting idea

5) add information or ideas

Add the discourse markers **despite**, **therefore**, **meanwhile**, **also** and **however** to the following paragraph so that it makes sense. Use each word only once.

I have become very concerned lately about the increase in local vandalism. I have

(a) .... heard complaints from many others. **(b)** ....,

I have decided to call a meeting. This will take place on Monday evening in the village hall.

(c) ...., I intend to get in touch again with my local councillor.

(d) .... his assurances, he and the rest of the councillors have so far failed

to take any action. **(e)** ...., I truly believe that when they see the strength of

local feeling, they will have to act.

Extend

Think about an issue that concerns you at your school or college. Imagine that you have been asked by your fellow students to write to the headteacher/principal about it. Note down five or six points you would like to make. Create a plan in the form of a spider diagram and then order the points.

Active Learning

Find a long article in a newspaper or magazine. List the paragraphs by topic to help you understand why a writer might start a new paragraph.

Revise 1

Draw lines to match the following terms with their functions in a text.

paragraph	The end or summing up.
topic sentence	A section of text marked by indentation or leaving a blank line.
discourse marker	A word or phrase that connects a sentence to the previous sentence or a paragraph to the previous paragraph.
conclusion	A sentence that introduces the topic or subject of a new paragraph.

Revise 2

Read the following paragraphs from a review of a school talent show. Work out the correct order so that the whole text makes sense and write the numbers 1 to 5 in the boxes to show the order.

a) One of the early highlights was surely Ms Grindley (Maths) and Mr O'Mara (PE) giving a crowd-pleasing, if slightly off-key, rendition of 'You're the One That I Want'. I don't know about you, but I think I detected some chemistry there – and I don't mean the sort you find in Dr Meredith's lab!

b) When it came to choosing a winner, however, there was no doubt about the audience's choice: Mr Jenkins' knife-throwing act. It was truly thrilling – and hats off to Mrs Burgess for volunteering to be his 'victim'. As she said, 'It was only a scratch.'

c) In contrast, we were treated to a number of very tuneful contributions from some of the students. I have to admit I'm not a fan of Disney tunes, but I couldn't fault the sincerity of the performers. Ronnie Ledowsky stood out, perhaps because he chose 'The Bare Necessities' from *The Jungle Book* rather than that dreadful dirge from *Frozen* (I counted four versions of that).

d) It was a great night and raised over £400 for the hospice. Let's hope it's the first of many.

e) Last Friday night, St Mungo's was delighted to host 'Mungo's Got Talent' to raise money for this year's chosen charity, The Elmswood Children's Hospice. The audience was thoroughly entertained by a huge variety of performances from both staff and students.

Look at the plan you made in the Extend activity on page 17. Write a strong opening paragraph for your letter, effectively introducing the issue that concerns you.

Extend

Write the rest of the letter, making sure that you include all the points from your spider diagram and connect them using discourse markers.

Active Learning

Look back at your old essays and practice exams. Check whether you have written in paragraphs that are effectively linked by discourse markers and clearly demarcated (preferably by an indentation of about 2cm or by leaving a blank line between paragraphs).

Revise 1

Four of the following sentences use personal pronouns correctly and four do not. Tick the ones that are correct and re-write the incorrect ones.

a) You and I really should get together for lunch. ☐

b) She asked Caroline and me to stay behind. ☐

c) Can you come with Ben and I to the park? ☐

d) You should all be very proud of your achievement. ☐

e) Me and Fran got the best marks. ☐

f) He said some really nice things about Kim and I. ☐

g) You are definitely my best friend. ☐

h) Tommy and me won the prize. ☐

....

....

....

....

Revise 2

Highlight or underline the Standard English word in the following sentences.

a) We were **standing** / **stood** under a tree when the rain started.

b) Could you bring me **them** / **those** cakes, please?

c) He **sneaked** / **snuck** in just in time.

d) She played **amazing** / **amazingly**.

e) I've already **forgot** / **forgotten** the tune.

f) Shakespeare **wrote** / **writ** *Julius Caesar*.

Re-write the following sentences using formal Standard English.

a) It were dead sick. I loved it.

b) You guys were much better than we was.

c) It was like you know mega scary.

d) They'd already gotten their scran and were sat at a table.

e) Ain't them dudes hot?

Extend

Write two or three paragraphs explaining:

a) why you should normally use Standard English in your writing

b) when it is acceptable not to do so.

Active Learning

Find an article that is not written entirely in Standard English in a magazine or newspaper or on a website. Think about why it has been written in this way and the effect on the reader.

Revise 1

Four of the following sentences use verb forms correctly and four do not. Tick the ones that are correct and re-write the incorrect ones.

a) We seen you in town the other day. ☐

b) I did the ironing before I left the house. ☐

c) We was really pleased with the way it went. ☐

d) They done nothing yesterday. ☐

e) They have done all their homework. ☐

f) I know because I saw them doing it. ☐

g) I were in all day. ☐

h) We were not given the correct instructions. ☐

Revise 2

Highlight or underline the Standard English word in the following sentences.

a) He **sung / sang** the whole song out of tune.

b) Do you mind if I **lay / lie** down for a bit?

c) She **gave / give** me a wonderful present.

d) They would **have / of gone / went** if they could.

e) I've already **ate / eaten** my dinner.

f) He has **sung / sang** in public a few times.

g) She has **spoke / spoken** to me a few times.

Re-write the following passage, using formal Standard English.

I'm gonna say this only once. After I seen her yesterday, I were dead upset. She were bang out of order, dissing me in front of all them kids. Nobody never spoke to me like that before. We was all in the yard like just chilling and she come over. 'I want a word with you guys,' she goes, dead aggressive like. Me and Gretchen were stood next to each other and we just lost it. I know we shouldn't of, but we did.

Extend

Imagine that you are a teacher who witnessed the incident above. Using Standard English, write a formal report about what happened in two or three paragraphs.

Active Learning

Watch or listen to a news/current affairs broadcast on television or the radio and make a note of the first ten examples of non-Standard English you hear. What would the Standard English forms have been?

Revise 1

If you choose to complete the narrative task in the exam, which of the following are acceptable?

a) a fictional story ☐

b) a newspaper article giving your opinion ☐

c) a description with no plot ☐

d) a true account of something that happened to you in the past ☐

Revise 2

Explain briefly why you might use the following in a story:

a) the first person

....

....

....

b) the third person

....

....

....

c) the past tense

....

....

....

d) the present tense

....

....

....

....

Imagine you have chosen to answer this question in your exam: 'Write about an event that changed someone's life forever'. Decide on the identity of the protagonist: either you, someone you know or an invented character. Make notes about the protagonist's character.

Extend

Still thinking about the question above, decide on a possible antagonist for the story and any other characters you might need. Give them names and make notes on them.

Revise 1

Think again about the story you would write in response to the question: 'Write about an event that changed someone's life forever'. Make notes on the following:

a) Where does the story begin?

b) Does the setting change during the story and, if so, how?

c) When is it set – in the past (if so, when?), in the future (if so, when?) or in the present day?

d) Will you write in chronological order? If not, how will you order the events?

Revise 2

Create a brief plan for your story by making notes for your:

a) exposition

b) inciting incident

c) turning point(s)

_____

_____

_____

d) climax

_____

_____

_____

e) coda (ending)

_____

_____

_____

Revise 3

Write a strong opening paragraph for your story, making sure you engage the interest of the reader.

_____

_____

_____

_____

_____

_____

_____

_____

_____

Extend

Write the rest of the story in a maximum of six paragraphs. Look back at your answers to 'Revise 2' to make sure your story is well-structured.

Active Learning

Make sure that you understand what is meant by the terms in Revise 2. Think about a well-known story and try to pinpoint those elements in the narrative.

Revise 1

If you choose the descriptive task in the exam, which of the following are acceptable?

a) an adventure story ☐

b) a discussion of issues associated with the picture ☐

c) a detailed description of the picture and scenes that are not in the picture ☐

d) a piece that focuses on description but includes some narrative ☐

Revise 2

Find three words which you could use instead of each of the following verbs and think about their precise meaning.

a) walk

_____

_____

_____

b) eat

_____

_____

_____

c) like

_____

_____

_____

d) dislike

e) speak

Find a photograph of yourself, preferably from a few years ago, and describe what you look like in it.

Extend

Continue your description from the Revise 3 task by writing two or three more paragraphs about what you looked like, how you felt and what the picture reminds you of. Use at least one metaphor and one simile.

Active Learning

Look at your response to the Extend task for 'Narrative Writing 2' and see whether you can improve it by adding some appropriate description.

Revise 1

Make brief notes about the room you are in now:

a) start with a general impression of the scene

_____

_____

_____

b) now focus on two or three particular details

_____

_____

_____

c) consider what the scene makes you feel or think about.

_____

_____

_____

_____

Revise 2

Using a noun and at least one adjective, make a note of at least two things in the room that you can:

a) see

_____

_____

b) hear

_____

_____

c) smell

_____

_____

d) taste

....

....

e) touch.

....

....

Note: Depending on the room you're in, you may not be able to complete all five.

Revise 3

Write a strong opening paragraph for a descriptive piece about the room you are in.

....

....

....

....

....

....

....

....

....

....

Extend

Write three or four additional paragraphs for your description, ensuring that they cover a range of ideas and are connected by discourse markers.

Active Learning

Go for a walk, taking in everything around you. When you get back, make some notes from memory about what you saw.

Revise 1

Which of the following might you be asked to write in Paper 2?

a) a letter to a newspaper ☐

b) an article for a magazine ☐

c) a short story ☐

d) an essay putting forward an argument ☐

e) an article for a broadsheet newspaper ☐

f) a speech for a school assembly ☐

Revise 2

Read the following tasks that you could be set in Paper 2:

a) Write a letter to the governing body of your school or college. ☐

b) Write an article for a teenage magazine or website. ☐

c) Write a letter on a current issue to a national newspaper. ☐

d) Write a topical article for a local newspaper. ☐

Decide which of the following statements about tone and language relates to each given task and write the numbers 1 to 4 in the correct boxes above.

1. Your language might be less formal when addressing this audience.

2. You should use precise references to local places and issues.

3. Your tone should be very polite.

4. You can express your opinion as strongly as you wish but you must use Standard English.

Explain briefly how the following could improve your non-fiction writing:

a) using discourse markers

b) presenting more than one point of view

c) using the first and second person

d) backing up your points with evidence

e) using anecdotes

f) using rhetorical questions.

Extend

Write two or three paragraphs about something that has recently made you angry. Make sure you use each of the following once: a rhetorical question, hyperbole and a list of three.

Active Learning

Read the letters page in a newspaper or magazine (print or online) to see what sort of issues people write about and how they express their views.

Revise 1

You have been asked to respond to the following statement: 'School holidays are far too long. They should be reduced to six weeks a year.'

In one sentence, say whether you agree or disagree with this statement and why.

....

....

....

Revise 2

In the table below, list five arguments in favour of reducing school holidays (pros) and five arguments against reducing school holidays (cons).

Pros	Cons

Write the first paragraph of an article responding to the statement in Revise 1. Use at least one of each of the following sentence types: simple, complex and compound.

Extend

Write three more paragraphs for the same article. In the first paragraph, develop your argument; in the second, give an opposing point of view; and in the third, give your counter-argument to that view.

Active Learning

Look again at the letters page in a newspaper or magazine and pick out words and expressions that effectively convey the writers' feelings about their subjects.

Revise 1

Below are some of the features you might use when writing a newspaper article or a letter. Sort them into the appropriate columns. Note that some of the features could be used in both.

your address   a headline   a strapline   a salutation   subheadings
paragraphs   a date

Newspaper article	Letter

Revise 2

Re-write the following informal letter using formal writing. Give it a more persuasive and courteous (polite) tone.

> Moloney,
>
> You've got to do something about our street. It's full of dog muck and other stuff. You need to get some guys in to clean it up now. If not, we'll all get sick. If you want our votes next time round, get off your bum and do something for a change.
>
> A well-wisher

_____

_____

_____

_____

_____

_____

_____

_____

_____

Write the opening paragraph of a letter to a local newspaper disagreeing with the opinion recently published in the paper that 'this town is in terminal decline'. Make sure you follow the conventions of letter writing.

Extend

Complete the letter by writing three or four more paragraphs. Try to make at least three separate points in support of your argument and include a personal anecdote.

Active Learning

Look in a newspaper (in print or online) for an 'opinion piece' about a topic that's in the news. Think about how the writer structures his/her argument and uses language to put it across.

Revise 1

Add the following words to the paragraph below so that it makes sense.

outrageous   assertion   generalisation   fortunately   complex
irresponsible   representative   attitude   anti-social   condition   acknowledge

The **(a)** .... that young people are responsible for the

(b) .... of the high street is an **(c)** ....

(d) .... Not all young people are **(e)** ...., whatever

Councillor Moloney might think. **(f)** ...., his views are no more

(g) .... of the **(h)** .... of the older generation than

the actions of a few **(i)** .... teenagers are of ours. The problem, as I'm sure

Mr Moloney will **(j)** .... when he stops playing to the gallery, is much more

(k) ....

Revise 2

Read the following phrases:

a) While that argument has some merit ...

b) Another worrying trend ...

c) On a recent visit to Framlington ...

d) But what can be done about it?

e) There are people who say that ...

f) This is not only nonsense: it is dangerous nonsense.

Indicate which phrase you could use for the following purposes by writing the appropriate number in the boxes above.

1) to introduce personal experience/an anecdote

2) to introduce a counter-argument

3) to reject (and belittle) a statement of opinion

4) to start making a new point

5) to introduce a possible solution to a problem

6) to acknowledge and explain the opinions of others

Write an anecdote that could be used as the opening for a speech to a meeting of local residents agreeing with the opinion that 'this town is in terminal decline'.

....

....

....

....

....

....

....

Extend

Complete the speech by writing three or four more paragraphs, covering a range of points and using discourse markers to connect them.

Active Learning

Look again at the article you found for the Active Learning task on page 37. Now see if you can find another article, whether in the same newspaper, a different paper or elsewhere on the internet, giving a different point of view on the same subject. Compare them and decide which one you find more convincing.

You are going to enter a creative writing competition.

Write a description of a child suggested by this picture.

Very quickly, note down some words and phrases that the picture brings to mind.

Plan your response to the question. Try to come up with four or five ideas, all inspired by the picture. Spend no more than five minutes on this.

Extend

Write your response to the question. Spend about 30 to 35 minutes on this.

Check

Spend five minutes checking your work. Check that:

- you have written in paragraphs
- you have used appropriate descriptive language and varied vocabulary
- your spelling, punctuation and grammar are correct.

Make corrections to your work by crossing out errors and clearly writing the correction above.

A magazine is looking for contributions to its creative writing section.

Write a description of a place suggested by this picture.

Revise 1

Very quickly, note down some words and phrases that the picture brings to mind.

....

....

....

....

....

....

....

Plan your response to the question. Try to come up with four or five ideas, all inspired by the picture. Spend no more than five minutes on this.

Extend

Write your response to the question. Spend about 30 to 35 minutes on this.

Check

Spend five minutes checking your work. Check that:

- you have written in paragraphs

- you have used appropriate descriptive language and varied vocabulary

- your spelling, punctuation and grammar are correct.

Make corrections to your work by crossing out errors and clearly writing the correction above.

Your local library is holding a creative writing competition.

Write a description of a place suggested by this picture.

Revise 1

Very quickly, note down some words and phrases that the picture brings to mind.

Plan your response to the question. Try to come up with four or five ideas, all inspired by the picture. Spend no more than five minutes on this.

Extend

Write your response to the question. Spend about 30 to 35 minutes on this.

Check

Spend five minutes checking your work. Check that:

- you have written in paragraphs

- you have used appropriate descriptive language and varied vocabulary

- your spelling, punctuation and grammar are correct.

Make corrections to your work by crossing out errors and clearly writing the correction above.

A local newspaper has asked you to contribute a piece of creative writing.

Write a descriptive piece suggested by this picture.

Revise 1

Very quickly, note down some words and phrases that the picture brings to mind.

....

....

....

....

....

....

Plan your response to the question. Try to come up with four or five ideas, all inspired by the picture. Spend no more than five minutes on this.

Extend

Write your response to the question. Spend about 30 to 35 minutes on this.

Check

Spend five minutes checking your work. Check that:

- you have written in paragraphs
- you have used appropriate descriptive language and varied vocabulary
- your spelling, punctuation and grammar are correct.

Make corrections to your work by crossing out errors and clearly writing the correction above.

You are going to enter a creative writing competition.

Write a story about an unexpected visitor.

Revise 1

a) Jot down your initial responses to the task.

b) Will you use a true incident or make up a story? Make some notes.

c) Who was the visitor and why was he/she unexpected? Make some notes.

d) Who is your protagonist? Make some notes.

e) Will you write in the third or first person?

Plan your response to the question. Try to come up with four or five ideas about what happens in your story and put them in order.

Spend no more than five minutes on this.

Extend

Write your response to the question.
Spend about 30 to 35 minutes on this.

Check

Spend five minutes checking your work. Check that:

- you have written in paragraphs

- you have used appropriate descriptive language and varied vocabulary

- your spelling, punctuation and grammar are correct.

Make corrections to your work by crossing out errors and clearly writing the correction above.

A magazine is looking for contributions to its creative writing section.

Write a story about two people who are reunited after a long time apart.

Revise 1

a) Jot down your initial responses to the task.

b) Will you use a true incident or make up a story? Make some notes.

c) Who are the people, why have they been apart, and why and how do they meet again? Make some notes.

d) Who is your protagonist? Make some notes.

e) Will you write in the third or first person?

Plan your response to the question. Try to come up with four or five ideas about what happens in your story and put them in order.

Spend no more than five minutes on this.

Extend

Write your response to the question.
Spend about 30 to 35 minutes on this.

Check

Spend five minutes checking your work.
Check that:

- you have written in paragraphs

- you have used appropriate descriptive language and varied vocabulary

- your spelling, punctuation and grammar are correct.

Make corrections to your work by crossing out errors and clearly writing the correction above.

Your local library is holding a creative writing competition.

Write a story entitled 'A New Beginning'.

Revise 1

a) Jot down your initial responses to the task.

b) Will you use a true incident or make up a story? Make some notes.

c) What is the new beginning? Make some notes.

d) Who is your your protagonist? Make some notes.

e) Will you write in the third or first person?

Plan your response to the question. Try to come up with four or five ideas about what happens in your story and put them in order.

Spend no more than five minutes on this.

Extend

Write your response to the question. Spend about 30 to 35 minutes on this.

Check

Spend five minutes checking your work. Check that:

- you have written in paragraphs

- you have used appropriate descriptive language and varied vocabulary

- your spelling, punctuation and grammar are correct.

Make corrections to your work by crossing out errors and clearly writing the correction above.

A local newspaper has asked you to contribute a piece of creative writing.

Write a story that begins, 'I opened the box.'

a) Jot down your initial responses to the task.

b) Will you use a true incident or make up a story? Make some notes.

c) Why did you open the box and what was in it? Make some notes.

d) Who is your protagonist? Make some notes.

e) Is it you or you are adopting a persona?

Plan your response to the question. Try to come up with four or five ideas about what happens in your story and put them in order.

Spend no more than five minutes on this.

Extend

Write your response to the question. Spend about 30 to 35 minutes on this.

Check

Spend five minutes checking your work. Check that:

- you have written in paragraphs
- you have used appropriate descriptive language and varied vocabulary
- your spelling, punctuation and grammar are correct.

Make corrections to your work by crossing out errors and clearly writing the correction above.

A local newspaper is holding a short story competition.

Write a story suggested by this picture.

Jot down some words and phrases that the picture suggests.

Decide whether to use a true incident or make up a story.

Think about your protagonist and whether to use a first- or third-person narrator.

Plan your response to the question. Try to come up with four or five ideas about what happens in your story and put them in order.

Spend no more than five minutes on this.

Extend

Write your response to the question. Spend about 30 to 35 minutes on this.

Check

Spend five minutes checking your work. Check that:

- you have written in paragraphs
- you have used appropriate descriptive language and varied vocabulary
- your spelling, punctuation and grammar are correct.

Make corrections to your work by crossing out errors and clearly writing the correction above.

'It is a growing trend for young people to ask others to sponsor them to go on expensive trips abroad, for example climbing Mount Kilimanjaro, in the name of charity. Why can't they just walk round the local park?'

Write a letter to a local newspaper in which you explain your point of view on this statement.

Revise 1

a) Highlight key words or phrases in the statement.

b) Very quickly, jot down some points agreeing with the statement.

c) Jot down some points disagreeing with the statement.

d) Decide whether you agree or disagree with the statement.

Plan your response to the question.

Try to come up with four or five ideas (including both points of view) and put them in order.

Spend no more than five minutes on this.

Extend

Write your response to the question.
Spend about 30 to 35 minutes on this.

Check

Spend five minutes checking your work.
Check that:

- you have written in paragraphs
- you have used appropriate language and varied vocabulary
- your spelling, punctuation and grammar are correct.

Make corrections to your work by crossing out errors and clearly writing the correction above.

'Taking a day off school and marching around the city centre is never going to help the environment. Staying in school and learning about it might.'

Write an article for a broadsheet newspaper in which you argue **for** or **against** this statement.

Revise 1

a) Highlight key words or phrases in the statement.

b) Very quickly, jot down some points agreeing with the statement.

....

....

....

....

....

c) Jot down some points disagreeing with the statement.

....

....

....

....

....

d) Decide whether you agree or disagree with the statement.

....

....

....

....

....

....

Plan your response to the question.

Try to come up with four or five ideas (including both points of view) and put them in order.

Spend no more than five minutes on this.

Extend

Write your response to the question.
Spend about 30 to 35 minutes on this.

Check

Spend five minutes checking your work.
Check that:

- you have written in paragraphs
- you have used appropriate language and varied vocabulary
- your spelling, punctuation and grammar are correct.

Make corrections to your work by crossing out errors and clearly writing the correction above.

'In this country, academic achievement is more valued than practical skills. Unless this changes, we will never have a successful economy.'

Write an article for a broadsheet newspaper in which you express your point of view on this statement.

Revise 1

a) Highlight key words or phrases in the statement.

b) Very quickly, jot down some points agreeing with the statement.

c) Jot down some points disagreeing with the statement.

d) Decide whether you agree or disagree with the statement.

Plan your response to the question.

Try to come up with four or five ideas (including both points of view) and put them in order.

Spend no more than five minutes on this.

Extend

Write your response to the question.
Spend about 30 to 35 minutes on this.

Check

Spend five minutes checking your work.
Check that:

- you have written in paragraphs

- you have used appropriate language and varied vocabulary

- your spelling, punctuation and grammar are correct.

Make corrections to your work by crossing out errors and clearly writing the correction above.

'Life today is very difficult for young people.'

Write a speech for a school debate in which you argue **for** or **against** this statement.

Revise 1

a) Highlight key words or phrases in the statement.

b) Very quickly, jot down some points agreeing with the statement.

c) Jot down some points disagreeing with the statement.

d) Decide whether you agree or disagree with the statement.

Plan your response to the question.

Try to come up with four or five ideas (including both points of view) and put them in order.

Spend no more than five minutes on this.

Extend

Write your response to the question.
Spend about 30 to 35 minutes on this.

Check

Spend five minutes checking your work.
Check that:

- you have written in paragraphs

- you have used appropriate language and varied vocabulary

- your spelling, punctuation and grammar are correct.

Make corrections to your work by crossing out errors and clearly writing the correction above.

'We would be a lot better off if the internet had never been invented.'

Write an article for a magazine in which you explain your point of view on this statement.

Revise 1

a) Highlight key words or phrases in the statement.

b) Very quickly, jot down some points agreeing with the statement.

c) Jot down some points disagreeing with the statement.

d) Decide whether you agree or disagree with the statement.

Plan your response to the question.

Try to come up with four or five ideas (including both points of view) and put them in order.

Spend no more than five minutes on this.

Extend

Write your response to the question.
Spend about 30 to 35 minutes on this.

Check

Spend five minutes checking your work.
Check that:

- you have written in paragraphs

- you have used appropriate language and varied vocabulary

- your spelling, punctuation and grammar are correct.

Make corrections to your work by crossing out errors and clearly writing the correction above.

'Childhood obesity is a major problem and is getting worse. However, we will not tackle it by banning adverts and taxing junk food.'

Write a letter to a broadsheet newspaper in which you give your response to this statement.

> Revise 1

a) Highlight key words or phrases in the statement.

b) Very quickly, jot down some points agreeing with the statement.

_____

_____

_____

_____

_____

c) Jot down some points disagreeing with the statement.

_____

_____

_____

_____

_____

d) Decide whether you agree or disagree with the statement.

_____

_____

_____

_____

_____

Plan your response to the question.

Try to come up with four or five ideas (including both points of view) and put them in order.

Spend no more than five minutes on this.

Extend

Write your response to the question.
Spend about 30 to 35 minutes on this.

Check

Spend five minutes checking your work.
Check that:

- you have written in paragraphs

- you have used appropriate language and varied vocabulary

- your spelling, punctuation and grammar are correct.

Make corrections to your work by crossing out errors and clearly writing the correction above.

'Nobody has the right to tell anybody else what to do or how to think.'

Write a speech for a school assembly expressing your opinion on this statement.

Revise 1

a) Highlight key words or phrases in the statement.

b) Very quickly, jot down some points agreeing with the statement.

....

....

....

....

....

....

c) Jot down some points disagreeing with the statement.

....

....

....

....

....

....

d) Decide whether you agree or disagree with the statement.

....

....

....

....

....

....

Plan your response to the question.

Try to come up with four or five ideas (including both points of view) and put them in order.

Spend no more than five minutes on this.

Extend

Write your response to the question.
Spend about 30 to 35 minutes on this.

Check

Spend five minutes checking your work.
Check that:

- you have written in paragraphs

- you have used appropriate language and varied vocabulary

- your spelling, punctuation and grammar are correct.

Make corrections to your work by crossing out errors and clearly writing the correction above.

'Schools and colleges have turned into exam factories. This is harmful to young people and does not improve their education. We should abolish all exams.'

Write an article for a broadsheet newspaper arguing **for** or **against** this statement.

Revise 1

a) Highlight key words or phrases in the statement.

b) Very quickly, jot down some points agreeing with the statement.

c) Jot down some points disagreeing with the statement.

d) Decide whether you agree or disagree with the statement.

Plan your response to the question.

Try to come up with four or five ideas (including both points of view) and put them in order.

Spend no more than five minutes on this.

Extend

Write your response to the question.
Spend about 30 to 35 minutes on this.

Check

Spend five minutes checking your work.
Check that:

- you have written in paragraphs
- you have used appropriate language and varied vocabulary
- your spelling, punctuation and grammar are correct.

Make corrections to your work by crossing out errors and clearly writing the correction above.

Answers

Pages 4–5

Revise 1

On Saturday I **whent** to the cinema with my **freind**. After we **bort are** tickets we saw a **women** who lives next door to me. She **sed** she had seen the movie and it was **grate** so she **woz** going to see it **agen**. She was **rite**. It was really good.

Correct spellings: went, friend, bought, our, woman, said, great, was, again, right

Revise 2

a) whose, who's, b) are, our, c) it's, its, d) you're, your, e) write, right, f) brake, break

Revise 3

a) keys, b) pianos, c) sheep, d) cacti, e) catches, f) wishes, g) chimneys, h) quantities, i) arenas, j) glasses, k) potatoes, l) soliloquies

Extend

I have decided to **wright** my autobiography. I have had a relatively short but, I think, **definately** interesting life. I never **new** who my mother and **farther wear** because I was abandoned on the steps of the **locale** hospital when I was only a few days old. **Fortunitely** I was found by a **sirgeon** who was doing a **nite** shift at the hospital and took me in. Otherwise, I dread to imagine what might have **occured**.

For **quiet** a long time my **storey** was in the paper almost every day. The nurses had **cristened** me 'Rosie' and **their** were frequent **appeels** for Rosie's parents to come forward but nobody ever did. Eventually I was **fosterd** and then adopted by my Mum and Dad. I love them but I have always been fascinated by my **wierd** background and so was very **exited** when I was approached by a television company who wanted to use my DNA to find out the truth.

Correct spellings: write, definitely, knew, father, were, local, fortunately, surgeon, night, occurred, quite, story, christened, there, appeals, fostered, weird, excited (18 in all)

Pages 6–7

Revise 1

a) advise, advice, b) where, were, we're, c) practice, practise, d) they're, there, their, e) flour, flower, f) stationery, stationary

Revise 2

a) permitted, b) greeted, c) travelled, d) revealed, e) regretted, f) visited, g) happened, h) entertained, i) cancelled, j) recurred, k) succeeded

Revise 3

a) accommodation, b) tragedy, c) privilege, d) diarrhoea, e) occasionally, f) successful, g) euphemistic, h) authoritative

Extend

a) 'i' before 'e' except after 'c' – but remember this is only for 'ee' sounds

and there are still some exceptions, such as 'seize'.

b) When the 'y' is preceded by a consonant, change the 'y' to 'i' and add 'es' (e.g. pity → pities, cherry → cherries). When the 'y' is preceded by a vowel, just add 's' (e.g. donkey → donkeys, boy → boys).

c) Always double the consonant for one-syllable words that end in a consonant after a short vowel (e.g. ban → banned, fret → fretting). For words of more than one syllable, double the final consonant if it is preceded by a vowel or the word consists of more than one syllable and the stress is placed on the second syllable (e.g. regret → regretted, occur → occurring).

However, if the final consonant is 'l', it is always doubled regardless of stress (e.g. travel → travelled) and if the final consonant is 'y' or 'w' it is never doubled (e.g. allow → allowed, play → played).

d) Add 'es' when a word ends in 's' (e.g. bus → buses), in a 'hissing' or 'buzzing' sound (e.g. glass → glasses, dash → dashes, quiz → quizzes), or in 'tch' (e.g. catch → catches).

e) Add 'es' (e.g. tomatoes) unless the word is of Italian origin (usually something related to music, e.g. pianos, piccolos).

Pages 8–9

Revise 1

Nothing could have prepared me for what happened next. **T**he researcher got in touch shortly after Christmas. **S**he told me that she had good news. **T**hey had found my birth mother. **I** was full of conflicting emotions. **I** really wasn't sure whether I wanted to know but I had started something I had to finish.

Revise 2

a) I **didn't** know it at the time but the car was **Jay's**.

b) We ordered pizzas from **Giorgio's** takeaway.

c) The **boys'** mums and dads all came to the **parents'** evening.

d) We **wouldn't** have bought the car if **we'd** known its age.

e) The **class's** marks were good but **weren't** the best **they'd** ever had.

Revise 3

Allie, who was the first person to get in touch, was extremely helpful. **S**he explained how I would get the test results, what they would mean and what to do next. **H**owever, she could not prepare me for everything. **S**he told me there was a match and that it was probably a sibling or child of my birth mother. **W**hat did that mean in practical terms? **A**ccording to Allie, it meant that the match, if he or she were willing, might tell me the truth. **A**mazing!

Extend

Commas should be used to demarcate subordinate clauses, which are clauses that add extra information and without which the sentence would still make sense. They are used to divide items in lists and can be used to introduce or end direct speech.

Pages 10–11

Revise 1

brackets	Put around additional bits of information in a sentence.
ellipsis	Used to show the omission of words from a sentence or to show a thought trailing off.
dash	Used to show an interruption to the train of thought.
inverted commas	Used to indicate speech, titles or quotations.

Revise 2

a) The candle flickered; the coals spluttered.

b) The house grew dark: the power had failed.

c) Despite the dim light, we carried on talking.

d) There was plenty to talk about: our plans for the holiday; what we were going to eat; and what would happen if power wasn't restored. (Commas would also be acceptable in this sentence.)

e) Finally, Jim, who was the oldest of the group, decided to look under the stairs for the fuse box.

f) 'There's a torch here,' he said, 'so I should be able to see what the problem is.'

Revise 3

It's (or '**it is**') quite a big house. **T**he owners rented it to us while they were away. Jim, who knew them quite well, had made all the arrangements. I **didn't** know anyone else there except Maria. **H**owever, they all seemed very pleasant. I'd had a bit of trouble finding it: it was quite dark when I got off the bus.

Extend

Sample answer:

Suddenly, we heard a strange noise.

'Was that you, Jim?' asked Alesha.

'What do you mean?' he asked.

'Someone made a noise,' she replied, 'and it must have been you.'

'I didn't make any noise,' Jim said, 'but I have found the torch.'

'If it wasn't you, it must have been a ghost,' whispered Gary, 'because it certainly wasn't any of us.'

'You're being silly,' Maria said angrily. 'There's no such thing as ghosts.' Then we heard it again.

(Remember to start a new paragraph for a new speaker.)

Pages 12–13
Revise 1
a) subject: we; main verb: ate; (direct) object: the pies.
b) subject: the massive dog; main verb: barked; preposition: at; (direct) object: the moon.
c) subject: all the plates; main verb: were washed; preposition: by; agent: Jim.
d) subject: nobody; main verb: likes; (direct) object: a know-all.
e) subject: Maria; main verb: found; (direct) object: the torch; preposition: in; (indirect) object: the bin.

Revise 2
a) The pies were bought (by us) at the corner shop.
b) The holiday was enjoyed by them all.
c) The last pie was eaten by the dog.
d) Before we left, we (or whoever cleaned the house) cleaned the house from top to bottom.
e) The noises scared me.
f) Someone (or a name) had filled the fridge with delicious snacks.

Revise 3
a) compound; b) complex; c) simple; d) minor

Extend
No definitive answer. Check that you have followed the instructions and highlight the different kinds of sentence you have used.

Pages 14–15
Revise 1
a) I chose that book **because** it is by my favourite author.
b) I had breakfast **before** I went to school.
c) I will not lend it to you **unless** you promise to give it back next week.
d) **Despite** revising for hours last night, I still couldn't do the test.

Revise 2
a) Mrs Arbuthnot, **who** lives next door, promised to help me revise.
b) I stayed up working until one o'clock, **which** turned out to be a mistake.
c) I'm going to meet Jo, **whom** ('**who**' is acceptable) I have known since primary school.
d) The apples, **which** I grew, were all sold. OR The apples **that** I grew were all sold.

Revise 3
The following answer is just one of many possibilities:

I walked to the nearest bus stop, where I met Jo. She told me that she couldn't go to town with me because her cat was ill and she had to take him to the vet's. Despite not really liking animals, I offered to go with her. She said that was very kind but she preferred to go alone. I got the impression that she was not telling the truth, so I left the bus stop and, feeling a bit guilty about not trusting her, decided to follow her.

Extend
No definitive answer. Check your answer and highlight the different kinds of sentence.

Pages 16–17
Revise 1
a), c), d) and e) are the correct answers.

Revise 2
a) As soon as (2: express passing time); b) however (4: introduce a contrasting idea); c) Furthermore (5: add information or ideas); d) Consequently (1: express cause and effect); e) Finally (3: give order or sum up)

Revise 3
a) also; b) Therefore; c) Meanwhile; d) Despite; e) However

Extend
No definitive answer.

Pages 18–19
Revise 1

paragraph	A section of text marked by indentation or leaving a blank line.
topic sentence	A sentence that introduces the topic or subject of a new paragraph.
discourse marker	A word or phrase that connects a sentence to the previous sentence or a paragraph to the previous paragraph.
conclusion	The end or summing up.

Revise 2
The correct order of the paragraphs is: e), a), c), b), d).

Revise 3
No definitive answer. Check your work for errors in spelling, grammar and punctuation.

Extend
No definitive answer. Check your work for errors in spelling, grammar and punctuation. Check that your letter follows a logical order and that your points are effectively linked.

Pages 20–21
Revise 1
a), b), d) and g) are correct.
c) Can you come with Ben and **me** to the park?
e) **Fran and I** got the best marks.
f) He said some really nice things about Kim and **me.**
h) Tommy and **I** won the prize.

Revise 2
a) standing; b) those; c) sneaked; d) amazingly; e) forgotten; f) wrote

Revise 3
Answers might include:
a) **It was really good.** I loved it.
b) You were much better than **we were**.
c) It was **really/very** scary.

d) They'd already **got** their **food** and were **sitting** at a table.
e) **Aren't those people attractive**?

Extend
Answers should include: a) in formal speech; in formal writing; usually in creative writing; b) when writing speech or dialogue in creative writing; when quoting someone who has not used Standard English; in informal writing addressed to a particular group, e.g. teenagers.

Pages 22–23
Revise 1
b), e), f) and h) are correct.
a) We **saw** you in town the other day.
c) We ~~were~~ really pleased with the way it went.
d) They **did** nothing yesterday.
g) I **was** in all day.

Revise 2
a) sang; b) lie; c) gave; d) have, gone; e) eaten; f) sung; g) spoken

Revise 3
There is often more than one formal Standard English word or expression that can be substituted for the non-Standard word or expression. Here is one way of changing the paragraph:

I am **going to** say this only once. After I **saw** her yesterday, I **was very** upset. She **was in the wrong, insulting** me in front of all **those children**. Nobody **has ever spoken** to me like that before. We **were** all in the yard, just **relaxing**, and she **came** over. 'I want a word with you guys,' she **said, really aggressively**. **Gretchen and I** were **standing** next to each other and we **lost our tempers**. I know we shouldn't **have**, but we did.

Extend
No definitive answer. Check that you have written in Standard English, using correct spelling, punctuation and grammar.

Pages 24–25
Revise 1
a) and d)

Revise 2
Answers might include:
a) It enables you to give an account of your own experiences; it helps to gain the empathy of the reader; it gives only one point of view.
b) It enables you to explore the minds of one or more characters; it gives an overview of the scene; it distances the reader from the protagonist(s).
c) It enables you to tell a story that has happened in the past; it enables you to reflect on what has happened.
d) It brings a sense of immediacy, involving the reader in the story.

Revise 3
No definitive answer, but answers might include references to the protagonist's age, gender, background, appearance and personality.

Extend

No definitive answer, but answers might include references to the name, age, gender, background, appearance and personality of any other characters in the story.

Pages 26–27

Revise 1

No definitive answer.

Revise 2

No definitive answer.

Revise 3

No definitive answer. Check your answer for grammar, spelling and punctuation.

Extend

No definitive answer. Check your answer for paragraphing, grammar, spelling and punctuation.

Pages 28–29

Revise 1

c) and **d)**

Revise 2

Answers could include:

a) stagger, amble, stride, totter, march, lope, waddle, trudge
b) devour, gobble, consume, nibble, munch, feast
c) love, adore, approve of, admire, relish, enjoy
d) hate, loathe, abhor, detest, despise, scorn
e) state, gabble, declare, exclaim, harangue, soliloquise

Revise 3

No definitive answer. Check that you have included some descriptive words and phrases, and that your spelling, punctuation and grammar are correct.

Extend

No definitive answer. Check that you have included imagery and descriptive words and at least one metaphor and one simile. Check that your spelling, punctuation and grammar are correct.

Pages 30–31

Revise 1

No definitive answer.

Revise 2

No definitive answer.

Revise 3

No definitive answer. Check that you have included descriptive words and that your spelling, punctuation and grammar are correct.

Extend

No definitive answer. Check that you have included some descriptive words and imagery. Check that your spelling, punctuation and grammar are correct.

Pages 32–33

Revise 1

All except **c)**

Revise 2

a) = 3; **b)** = 1; **c)** = 4; **d)** = 2

Revise 3

Answers might include:

a) They help to guide the reader through the argument.
b) It helps to show that you have considered both sides and helps to make your argument look more reasonable.
c) The first person can show your commitment and personal involvement; the second person can make the reader feel more involved with the subject.
d) It adds weight and authority to your arguments.
e) It can help to engage and maybe entertain the reader.
f) They can make readers or listeners engage with the subject by considering their own answers.

Extend

There is no definitive answer. Check that you have followed the instructions and check your spelling, punctuation and grammar.

Pages 34–35

Revise 1

No definitive answer.

Revise 2

Answers might include: **Pros:** pupils can forget what they have learnt over the holidays; they could learn a lot more if they were in school more; long holidays are inconvenient for parents; teachers are paid for doing nothing during this time; children may get into trouble if they have nothing to occupy them in the holidays; **Cons:** rest and recreation are important for children's development; teachers need time to recover and to prepare; summer holidays have to be long so families can go on holiday; pupils often revise or go to extra classes during the holidays; holidays give children the opportunity to do other useful things, such as part-time work or educational trips.

Revise 3

No definitive answer. Check that you have followed the instructions. Check your spelling, grammar and punctuation.

Extend

No definitive answer. Check that you have followed the instructions. Check your spelling, grammar and punctuation.

Pages 36–37

Revise 1

Newspaper article	Letter
a headline	your address
a strapline	a salutation
subheadings	a date
paragraphs	paragraphs

Revise 2

There are many possible answers. Below is one example.

Dear Mr Moloney,

I would like to bring to your attention the state of the street where I live. It has become blighted not only by litter of various sorts, but also by dog faeces. I am sure you will agree that it is about time the street was thoroughly cleaned. If left, it will undoubtedly create health problems for the residents. May I gently suggest that, if you do not act quickly, you may well lose our support in the forthcoming election.

Yours sincerely
AJ Harbinger

Revise 3

No definitive answer. Check your spelling, punctuation and grammar.

Extend

No definitive answer. Check that you have followed the instructions. Check your spelling, punctuation and grammar.

Pages 38–39

Revise 1

a) assertion, b) condition, c) outrageous, d) generalisation, e) irresponsible/anti-social, f) Fortunately, g) representative, h) attitude, i) anti-social/irresponsible, j) acknowledge, k) complex

Revise 2

a) = 2; b) = 4, c) = 1, d) = 5, e) = 6, f) = 3

Revise 3

No definitive answer. Check your spelling, punctuation and grammar.

Extend

No definitive answer. Think about whether your style is appropriate for your audience. Check your spelling, punctuation and grammar.

Pages 40–73

Exam Practice

Use the mark scheme to self-assess your strengths and weaknesses. Work up from the bottom, putting a tick by things you have fully accomplished, a ½ by skills that are in place but need securing, and underlining areas that need particular development. The estimated grade boundaries are included so you can assess your progress towards your target grade.

Grade	AO5 Content and Organisation (C&O) (24 marks)	AO6 Technical Accuracy (TA) (16 marks)
7+ C&O (19–24 marks) TA (13–16 marks)	Communication is convincing and engaging. Its tone, style and register are convincingly matched to audience and purpose. The vocabulary is varied and extensive and there is conscious crafting of linguistic devices. There is a varied and effective use of structural features. There are fluently linked paragraphs with integrated markers. Writing is engaging and includes a range of well-developed, complex ideas.	Sentences are consistently secure and accurately demarcated. There is a wide range of accurate punctuation. A full range of sentence forms is used for effect. Standard English is used consistently and appropriately with secure control of complex grammatical structures. A high level of accuracy in spelling includes ambitious vocabulary. Vocabulary is extensive and ambitious.
5–6 C&O (13–18 marks) TA (9–12 marks)	This answer communicates clearly. Its tone, style and register are clearly matched to audience and purpose. The vocabulary is chosen for effect and there is a variety of effective linguistic devices. There is an effective use of structural features. There are coherent paragraphs and a range of discourse markers. Writing is engaging with ideas clearly linked.	Sentences are mostly securely and accurately demarcated. There is a range of, usually accurate, punctuation. Varied sentence forms are used for effect. Standard English is used appropriately with mostly controlled grammatical structures. Complex and irregular words are usually spelt accurately. Vocabulary is increasingly sophisticated.
3–4 C&O (7–12 marks) TA (5–8 marks)	This answer communicates with some success. It shows an attempt, perhaps sustained, to match tone, style and register to audience and purpose. The vocabulary is varied and there is some use of linguistic devices. There is some use of structural features. There is some attempt at paragraphing and some use of discourse markers. Several relevant ideas are linked.	Sentences are usually securely and sometimes accurately demarcated. There is a range of controlled punctuation. There is an attempt at varying sentence forms. There is some use of Standard English with some control of agreement. Some complex words are spelt accurately. Vocabulary is varied.
1–2 C&O (1–6 marks) TA (1–4 marks)	This answer communicates in a simple way. It shows simple awareness of matching tone, style and register to audience and purpose. The vocabulary is simple. There may be some evidence of structural features. There may be some attempt at paragraphing. One or two ideas may be linked in a simple way.	Sentences are occasionally demarcated. There is some punctuation. Sentence forms are simple. There is some use of Standard English with limited agreement. Basic spelling is accurate. Vocabulary is simple.

Below are some of the ideas that might be included in your responses. However, bear in mind that the content of the best answers will be very varied and sometimes highly original.

Pages 40–41

Ideas might include: the happiness and joy on the child's face; the connotations of the painting; the colours in the scene; childhood innocence; the secure environment; some personal memories of early childhood; the child's perception of the world; the challenge of understanding a child's mind; what her appearance might tell us; things that might be inferred about her life and her background outside the picture; or it could be a description of a completely different child.

Pages 42–43

Ideas might include: the season; weather and temperature; sounds and smells suggested by the picture; where the place is; a personal memory of woods and/or winter; a sense of mystery; magic; loneliness; beauty; what lies beyond the picture; how the scene might change in different seasons; or a description of another place prompted by something in the picture.

Pages 44–45

Ideas might include: details in the scene; the evidence of human habitation; what kind of people live/lived there; smells, sounds and tastes suggested by the picture; the wider location of the scene; the haunting atmosphere; the period of the house; what the objects tell us about the time and place; a description of a wider area including the rest of the room/the house; or a description

of a completely different room inspired by looking at the picture.

Pages 46–47

Ideas might include: smells, sounds, feelings and tastes suggested by the picture; a sense of the wider setting, e.g. a farm; the contrast between cow and calf; the relationship between them; feelings and moods inspired in the onlooker; a contrast between rural idylls and the reality of farm life; or a description of different animals, people or places prompted by looking at the picture.

Pages 48–49

Ideas might include: the identity of the visitor: a long-lost friend or relative, a police officer or other official, someone with good news, someone with bad news, the protagonist's reaction to the visitor; the relationship between them; what the visitor does; the effect of the visitor's actions; serious or humorous consequences of the visit; how the visit changed the protagonist.

Pages 50–51

Ideas might include: the identities of the two people; their backgrounds; similarities and differences between them; what they used to be like; how they have changed; how they react to each other; why they lost touch; whether the meeting is deliberate or accidental; how it changes their lives; what happens next; funny, sad or tragic consequences; the narrator's/protagonist's reflections on the events.

Pages 52–53

Ideas might include: a move to a new house or school; a new relationship; an

opportunity; a change in personality; whether the new beginning is welcome; the reactions of the protagonist; the reactions of others; the events that follow the new beginning; amusing or serious consequences; the ultimate outcome of the change; reflections on the experience.

Pages 54–55

Ideas might include: what the box is like; why it is opened; what is inside it: an object of value and what the character(s) do with it, a document of some kind; whether or not the character(s) should have opened the box; what they do next; humorous or serious consequences of the action; unexpected outcomes; the effect on people of the act; the narrator's reflections on what has happened.

Pages 56–57

Ideas might include: where the station is; who the people in the picture are; where they are going; what they have done before this moment; what they will do afterwards; what other characters might be involved; how their (or somebody else's) actions change things; the consequences of their actions; the effect of the events.

Pages 58–59

Ideas agreeing with the statement might include: question over where the money goes (do they pay for their own travel?); local events would encourage more participation and attract more publicity; it depends what they are raising money for; travelling by air is bad for the environment; it's more about virtue signalling/showing off than helping others; there are plenty of challenging things to do nearer home.

Ideas disagreeing with the statement might include: anything that raises money for charity should be encouraged; a high-profile achievement would attract more money than just walking around a park; young people should be praised for doing something different; the experience will have benefits for the health and character of those doing it; there is room for many different ways of raising money (not just 'either or').

Pages 60–61

Ideas agreeing with the statement might include: those who go on marches may be ill-informed; they might just want a day off school (would they do it in the holidays?); those who organise the marches are using the young people for their own ends; the organisers over-simplify the issues; demonstrations in the UK will have little or no effect on the countries mostly responsible for climate change, e.g. China and India; Western governments are already doing a lot; the demonstrations disrupt people's lives and could alienate them; would they be allowed out of school to demonstrate about other, more controversial issues?; young people would become better informed by studying issues and discussing them rationally rather than listening to rabble-rousing speeches.

Ideas disagreeing with the statement might include: it is good for young people to get involved in action about things that concern them; the issue is of huge importance and should be brought to people's attention; high-profile protests can make governments and individuals act; getting involved can be more valuable educationally than spending an ordinary day in school; the young people might become more aware of the effects of their own behaviour and change it; it is wrong to be cynical about the motives of organisers and protestors.

Pages 62–63

Ideas agreeing with the statement might include: there is a skills shortage in the UK; productivity in manufacturing needs to improve and focusing on academic qualifications will not help to achieve this; many degrees are of little value in getting people jobs, whereas apprenticeships do help; huge increases in higher education numbers may keep people off the unemployment figures but actually devalues degrees; it is short sighted to rely on foreign workers to make up for skills shortages; many people are more suited to practical work but feel pressured to go to university; governments need to work to make technical and vocational subjects more attractive.

Ideas disagreeing with the statement might include: degrees are not just about getting jobs but also about broadening the mind; it is possible to have a degree and to be practical; it is wrong for governments to force people down a certain route; many governments in the past have tried and failed to increase the uptake of technical and vocational subjects; a successful economy is driven by ideas, research and

creative thinking, as developed in academic institutions; it is important that practical skills and academic achievement are not seen as opposites.

Pages 64–65

Ideas agreeing with the statement might include: young people are under a lot of pressure to succeed academically, not always for their own benefit; technology has introduced stresses that did not exist before; there has been an increase in mental health problems; young people are financially worse off than previous generations because of student debts, high house prices, etc; materialism and consumerism put pressure on people; communities breaking down and challenges to traditions/beliefs leave young people without moral certainty or a sense of belonging.

Ideas disagreeing with the statement might include: exam pressure is nothing new and is just a part of growing up; nobody has a stress-free life; technology and scientific advances have, in many ways, made life easier than it used to be; some problems, such as those relating to mental health, only appear to be increasing because of changes in awareness, acceptance and definitions; many young people have a lot more to spend than previous generations and are heavily subsidised by their parents – they expect too much; young people today have a lot more freedom to choose their own beliefs and lifestyles.

Pages 66–67

Ideas agreeing with the statement might include: harm to people's mental health; the spreading of unrealistic aspirations; its use as a political platform, especially for extremist and terrorist groups; its addictive effect, particularly for young people; opportunities it might give for surveillance; people living life through others; its role in encouraging a global monoculture at the expense of tradition and diversity.

Ideas disagreeing with the statement might include: its use in spreading information and education; its use in entertainment; its use as a tool for keeping in touch with people; how it encourages exposure to, and understanding of, other ways of life; the fact that it is up to individuals whether they use it for good or ill; how it makes life easier in many ways, e.g. booking holidays or transferring documents; how it might encourage internationalism for the good of the world.

Pages 68–69

Ideas agreeing with the statement might include: discussion of what is/is not banned or taxed; taxes make things more expensive but do not necessarily put people off them; how do we decide what to ban and where do we stop?; these solutions over-simplify the problems; the problems are too deeply rooted to be solved so easily; individuals (parents and children) should take responsibility for their own health; only eating less and taking more exercise can really help; governments should focus on education rather than punishment; the

people who suffer most from such measures are the poorest.

Ideas disagreeing with the statement might include: the problem is so severe that drastic measures are needed; advertising is insidious and targets vulnerable groups; children are easily influenced; making some foods more expensive might persuade people to buy cheaper, healthier options; taxes and bans are not the whole solution but can be part of it; revenues from taxes could help research and education.

Pages 70–71

Ideas agreeing with the statement might include: individual liberty is a basic right; we should have the right to express our views but not impose them on others; those in authority often assume their views are correct and expect others to follow; totalitarian regimes keep power by censorship and imposing uniform behaviour; if people are not allowed to express their views nothing will ever be challenged or changed; having ideas and behaviour imposed can have unintended consequences, such as driving people to crime or terrorism.

Ideas disagreeing with the statement might include: if children are not told what to do or think, they cannot develop normally; there must be ideas in society about what is acceptable and unacceptable; what is the difference between 'telling someone what to think' and expressing a strongly held view?; if people were allowed to do whatever they liked, there would be chaos; all societies need to find a balance between order and freedom; the problem is finding the balance and statements like the one above do not help.

Pages 72–73

Ideas agreeing with the statement might include: too many exams have a damaging effect on health; schools put too much emphasis on exams and 'teach to the test'; some people are not suited to exams and are made to feel like failures; emphasis on exams makes the curriculum too narrow; other qualities apart from academic achievement are not valued; exams stifle creativity and original thinking; exams put too much focus on measuring achievement and not enough on improvement.

Ideas disagreeing with the statement might include: without exams we would not know what children have learnt and so would be less able to help them improve; other methods of assessment are too open to abuse (hence the abolition of coursework in GCSEs); a certain amount of stress is helpful and exams help students to focus; it is important for employers to know what job applicants can and cannot do; exams in themselves do not lead to a narrowing of the curriculum as exams can be taken in a huge range of subjects; far from stifling creativity and original thinking, exams give students opportunities to express themselves and work out problems without distraction.

Notes

Snap up other workbooks from Collins:

9780008355265

9780008355272

9780008355289

9780008355296

9780008355302

9780008355319

9780008355326

9780008355333

Browse online at

collins.co.uk/revision